INNOVATIONS

Key to Business Success

INNOVATIONS

Key to Business Success

DAVID P. SORENSEN, PH.D.

CRISP PUBLICATIONS

Editor-in-Chief: *William F. Christopher*

Managing Editor: *Kathleen Barcos*

Editor: *Kay Keppler*

Cover Design: *Kathleen Barcos*

Cover Production: *Russell Leong Design*

Book Design & Production: *London Road Design*

Printer: *Bawden Printing*

Library of Congress Card Catalog Number 97-65796

ISBN 1-56052-431-6

CONTENTS

INTRODUCTION

The successful company of the future must understand how people really work and how technology can help them work more effectively. As managers come to recognize this, they can begin to search out the best practices necessary to establish a truly innovative culture that can serve well into the twenty-first century.

This is why many visitors representing business, academia, and government travel to St. Paul, Minnesota, to hear 3M's innovation story. Like 3M's leaders, these men and women realize that consistent innovation leads to long-term organizational vitality. They are looking for ways to create and sustain an innovative environment in their own organizations.

The total return to an organization from investing in creativity and innovation goes far beyond new products, new processes, or new marketing programs. Benefits that are hard to measure may well result in the biggest return. For example, employee morale tends to remain high or improve in an innovative organization. In this stimulating environment, employees, members of the organization, look upon heavy workloads as interesting challenges instead of burdens of drudgery.

When viewed from within an organization that annually is judged as one of industry's most admired, innovation and the establishment of an innovative culture are not nearly as complex as one might think. Most employees,

and especially innovators, have a well-defined set of
expectations of management and the company. Once
these expectations are fulfilled, people produce outstanding
results.

I.

ESTABLISHING AND ENHANCING AN INNOVATIVE ORGANIZATION

3M'S EXPECTATIONS ABOUT THE role of innovation are clearly stated in the company's vision statement and principles of management. 3M's vision is "to be recognized as the most innovative enterprise in the world and the preferred supplier for the products and services that we provide." This broad concept applies not only to 3M technical employees, but also to all other 3M employees, irrespective of location or job.

Innovation is expected in every functional area, not just in new products, which are "3M's engine for growth." These functional areas include marketing programs, manufacturing practices, delivery of products to the customer, human resource policies, as well as anything and everything else.

In 1944, William L. McKnight (3M President, 1929–1949; CEO 1949–1966) drafted the following management policy to formally establish the importance of innovation:

As our business grows, it becomes increasingly necessary to delegate responsibility and to encourage men and women to exercise their initiative. This requires considerable tolerance. Those men and women to whom we delegate authority and responsibility, if they are good people, are going to want to do their jobs their own way.

Mistakes will be made. But if a person is essentially right, the mistakes he or she makes are not as serious as the mistakes management will make if it undertakes to tell those in authority exactly how they must do their jobs.

Management that is destructively critical when mistakes are made kills initiative; and it's essential that we have people with initiative if we are to continue to grow.

3M Principles of Management

McKnight's confidence in 3M's employees led to a working environment in which creativity and risk-taking were—and continue to be—encouraged. Three powerful principles of management are followed.

- Promote entrepreneurship and the freedom to pursue innovative ideas.

- Adhere to uncompromising honesty and integrity.

- Preserve individual identity.

For more than 70 years, the tradition and value of innovation have been emphasized and enhanced throughout 3M. Today, innovation is the cornerstone of 3M's culture and a key feature of the company's success in global markets.

The 3M innovative culture and its "new-product machine" are responsible for introducing almost 500 new products each year to the global marketplace. More than 30% of sales come from products less than four years old.

> *Creativity requires the freedom to consider unthinkable*
> *alternatives, to doubt the worth of cherished practices.*
> John W. Gardner

Getting Started

The unwritten rule of business success today is that you can't achieve high performance without innovation. A corollary is this: To be truly innovative, managers must have the courage to take risks.

Once an organization decides to establish an innovative culture, or enhance its current innovative culture, it must continuously encourage and nurture all of the processes that support innovation. Innovation requires constant attention if it is to flourish and deliver the expected results. A warning: Paying lip service to innovation is worse than ignoring it. Failure to support what you claim to want produces only frustration and a high level of dissatisfaction. Innovation requires a resolute will to continue in spite of inevitable problems and failures.

Thus, to foster a climate of innovation, managers must set expectations, support, champion, recognize, and reward innovation. Managers must keep trying new ways to remove barriers and reduce the frustrations endemic to organizational bureaucracy.

To establish and maintain an environment conducive to innovation and creativity, management must act. The time-proven list of musts is long and covers all aspects of organizational activities. Here is a sampling of such actions.

- Encourage innovation across every function in the organization.

- Set corporate expectations for innovation and creativity.

- Develop and use strategies that drive innovation.

- Provide resources, time, and encouragement (15% rule).

- Ask employees what they need and give it to them.

- Share best practices and ideas.

- Celebrate successes and have fun together.

- Use formal award and recognition programs.

- Use mentors to instill creativity and innovation.

- Get informal—relax dress codes, remove barriers in approval processes, use first names, communicate better.

- Encourage the use of tools to improve innovation—books, courses, idea sessions, focus panels.

When developing new products:

- Use cross-functional teams from the beginning of a project.
- Get laboratory employees into the customers' shops and marketplaces.
- Create a career path for innovators.
- Use failures as learning experiences.
- Learn from the experts.

This list could go on and on. Fortunately, it can be broken down into seven major categories that can be covered separately.

1. Expectations
2. Communication
3. Freedom
4. Sponsorship
5. Informality
6. Supportive Management
7. Environment

The following sections briefly explore these seven categories and suggest ways of enhancing or establishing innovative processes in any organization.

Expectations

An organization cannot develop overnight a culture that supports and rewards innovative practices. Furthermore, it can never develop one unless all employees truly believe that creative thinking is a big part of their jobs. To establish the innovative process requires the full dedication and participation of everyone in the organization, especially senior management.

The entire process must begin with a clearly articulated vision and mission for the company. State objectives and implement programs to enforce the idea that innovation is everyone's job. Build that expectation into goals, strategies, and operating principles for the company. Do it also for individual departments, functions within departments, project and program planning, recognition programs, and performance evaluations for individuals and teams. Industrial firms especially should focus on the laboratories. Set specific new-product objectives. Establish—and use—productivity measurements.

State expectations in terms that employees understand and to which they can relate. Expect each employee to know how his or her job relates to company performance. People like to contribute—to feel that their skills, experiences, and capabilities are recognized and valued. Remember, your employees are the ones who can make a difference. Give them the freedom they need to meet your expectations.

An innovative organization is not hierarchical. Don't expect employee commitment if you persist in controlling instead of empowering. The anxiety you'll feel from lack of control will drain away with every unexpected breakthrough.

I was successful because you believed in me.
Ulysses S. Grant to Abraham Lincoln

Communication

Communication about innovation begins when the CEO establishes a clear, written philosophy that spells out the importance of innovation and creativity—and the company's absolute commitment to these values. This message needs to be communicated to all levels of the organization at every opportunity. Use signs and posters, articles in internal publications, product advertising, even slogans on coffee cups. By every means possible, let employees know that innovation and creativity are expected—and appreciated.

Establish and promote formal and informal communication lines between employees and all levels of management. The 3M Technical Forum is an example of how this can be done.

The 3M Technical Forum

The Technical Forum was founded in the early 1950s specifically to enhance two-way communication between laboratory employees and top management.

All technical employees belong to the forum, which is represented to management by the Technical Forum Senate. This body consists of a senator from each laboratory or technical group and a slate of officers elected by the general membership. The senate meets monthly to address issues of importance or interest to its members. These might include the sharing of technology and best practices among laboratories. The senate helps build informal communication networks among technical employees.

The senate also sponsors *chapters*, which are communication vehicles in technical disciplines that loosely correspond with 3M's core technical competencies. Employees in a discipline are encouraged to attend quarterly meetings of the chapters, where they will hear presentations by technical experts both from within and outside the company and share information about their own research interests and technical advances. Currently, 24 chapters operate in the 3M Technical Forum. Typical examples include the Adhesive/Adhesion Chapter, the Imaging Chapter, the Interfacial Sciences Chapter, and the Polymer Chapter.

The Annual Event is another interesting and effective communication method sponsored by the Technical Forum. The event is a mini-technology trade show. Each 3M laboratory has a booth where scientists can display—with poster boards, videos, and demonstrations—their most exciting new technologies or new products. This event lasts two-and-one-half days, and all Technical Forum members and their marketing counterparts are invited to attend, observe, and discuss. The Annual Event also is an excellent mechanism for assuring transfer of technology from one 3M laboratory to another.

Other Communication Organizations

Other organizations at 3M facilitate communication and share best practices among functions. Examples include the Technical Council (comprised of all laboratory heads in the company), the Manufacturing Council (all manufacturing heads), the Marketing Council (all marketing heads in the company), and the Executive Conference (all 3M executive personnel).

Freedom

The 15% Rule

Freedom is an essential ingredient of an innovative environment and culture. 3M's *15% rule* is central in its communication of freedom to employees. The rule says that technical employees may spend 15% of their time on projects of their own choosing—with only one stipulation. Whatever the idea or project, it must have potential commercial value for 3M. Experience teaches that some of these projects may produce blockbuster ideas. Our family of Post-it® Repositionable Notes began life as a 15% project.

To maintain an atmosphere of freedom, managers need to keep asking their employees what they need to be innovative and creative, and to get it for them.

Empowerment

Empowerment is the most important step that management can take as it builds or enhances an innovative culture. A 3M chairman now retired, Lewis W. Lehr, was fond of emphasizing this point with an aphorism. He said, "If you build fences around people, you get sheep, and you can't keep growing with sheep."

" I THINK DAVE TAKES A LITTLE NAP
EVERY DAY AFTER LUNCH. "

Figure 1.   Freedom to innovate (©3M)

Empowered employees accept more responsibility and more readily take risks than workers who are tightly controlled. However, it is necessary to keep telling employees they are free to make their own decisions.

Informality

Informality and the encouragement of a seamless organization also convey a feeling of freedom. Minimize

red tape and bureaucracy. If you haven't already done
so, adopt informal dress. Operate on a first name basis
regardless of level. Use matrix management instead of a
hierarchical approach. Depend on cross-functional teams
because they are more likely to transform an innovative
idea into reality. These steps are as effective as pulling
down the walls that physically separate managers from
their employees in a traditional business environment.
(If your physical barriers can't be trumpeted down like
the walls of Jericho, get out from behind them and learn
to "manage by walking around.")

Accepting Failures

Management—particularly upper management—needs
to be reminded regularly that not every new program will
succeed. There will be failures, and acceptance of failure
encourages risk taking. Without risk taking, innovation
and creativity are stifled, and success slips out of reach.
Also management needs to recognize that it takes time
and patience to create an environment in which failure is
viewed as a necessary byproduct of aggressive innovation
and not an object for punishment.

At 3M, the freedom to pursue innovative ideas is
guaranteed and encouraged by the first of three management principles developed during the decades of leadership provided by William L. McKnight, long-time president and CEO. This simple statement of a McKnight
belief served as a cornerstone for the development and
enhancement of an innovative culture that has survived
for more than 70 years.

*The first principle is the promotion of entrepreneurship
and insistence upon freedom in the workplace
to pursue innovative ideas.*

William L. McKnight
Former 3M President and CEO

Sponsorship

Outstanding managers—the men and women who repeat-
edly succeed in innovative efforts—are those who have
learned to bet on people, not just on numbers. They know
that innovative employees are self-motivated, can find their
way around obstacles, and can see possibilities invisible to
those with their noses to a grindstone of ordered and controlled activity. As sponsors of innovation, outstanding
managers offer their people:

- Challenge
- Responsibility with accountability
- Resources
- Reward

Challenge

Challenging work is the first ingredient of innovation. Every program must offer challenge, and the reason
for undertaking the program must be obvious to all participants. State objectives at the beginning, leaving no room
for ambiguity.

Responsibility and Resources

The second and third ingredients are responsibility with accountability and proper resourcing. Empowered employees make things happen. Give employees the task and the resources to accomplish their tasks, and then get out of the way. Set the tone and give the freedom. Given free choice, employees rarely assume too much responsibility. In fact, the real challenge is getting them to accept all of the responsibility that you are willing to delegate.

Reward

Rewards are essential. Don't wait until a program is completed before rewarding an individual or team. Project milestones and other "natural breaks" provide excellent opportunities for celebration. Even programs that fail can be celebrated if they've been valuable learning experiences. A *postmortem* on every program—success or failure—can provide extremely useful insights that can help make future programs more successful.

Rewards or celebrations need not be elaborate and expensive. Simple recognition by "the boss" for a job well done works best. Coffee parties or other small informal gatherings of the group are ideal opportunities to say, "Thank you." Major achievements deserve a dinner or a banquet with spouses and other important guests. Nothing is a better motivator than public recognition in the presence of other colleagues and associates.

Companies can do others things to sponsor innovation. For example, an industrial firm can establish small new-product groups within each of its business unit laboratories. Focus these little centers of innovation exclusively on new products, keep them out of the fire-fighting activities of the daily business, and let them help build the business through new products. With a well-defined mission, these small groups can focus on the business of innovating.

When hiring, look for people who are creative, have broad interests, are highly self-motivated, know how to get things done and, most of all, are open-minded problem-solvers. Then plant them in an environment that encourages them to expand their ideas. Be patient and keep in mind that your actions speak louder than your words—and that it takes time to transform ideas into innovations.

Informality

Informality in working relationships is critical for innovation to flourish. An atmosphere of partnership and cooperation is established or maintained by following some simple guidelines.

- Blur all lines on the organization charts while talking up the concept of a truly seamless company.

- Use first names and forget titles.

- Implement a casual dress code.

- Promote communication.

- Use matrix, instead of hierarchical, management.

- Make sure cross-functional teams contain at least one member from each key organizational function.

- If team members cannot be located at the same physical place, connect them electronically.

- Sponsor gatherings and organizations that promote transfer of best practices.

- Make management available for "talks" and informal reviews with employees in all functions and at all levels.

- Give employees a way to communicate easily with the top.

As with most of the other ideas presented in this book, these suggestions must be reinforced through continual repetition.

> *The way to get things done is not to mind*
> *who gets the credit of doing them.*
> Benjamin Jowett

Supportive Management

Managers who expect to inspire employees to be innovative must talk about innovation continuously, express expectations clearly, and follow through with actions. One way the people do this at 3M is through its Genesis Program. Laboratory employees are encouraged to submit ideas for new products or technologies to a review panel of management and senior technical experts. Ideas judged to have the greatest technical soundness, future sales potential, and strategic fit with business objectives receive corporate funding. New products, patents, and technical publications result from this innovation-supporting program. The biggest benefit, however, has been a noticeable increase in morale among technical employees.

Unfortunately, it's far easier to destroy an innovative culture than to build one. Employees continually evaluate management's performance in following through on its stated expectations. Everyone, especially members of management, must be on guard at all times to avoid communicating the wrong message. Here are a few examples of signals that management must avoid:

- "It'll never work!"

- "We explored that thoroughly 10 years ago!"

- "OK, if we can get somebody else to pay for it!"

- "We're too shorthanded to work on blue sky ideas!"

- "It's not in the business plan!"

- "It's not your job to talk to customers!"

- "Interesting, but let's see what the top brass think of it!"

- "Hey, I like that idea! Let's see what Joe can do with it!"

The old axiom, *Actions speak louder than words,* is especially true in dealing with innovators. Being naturally suspicious, technical innovators watch management's every move. If, for example, a high-risk program is to be phased out, displaced employees must be assigned to other significant programs and not terminated or placed in dead-end jobs. To do otherwise sends all employees a clear signal to respond not to the company's exhortations, but to the company's actions. This is a sure way to keep your best people from volunteering for anything but a sure bet, and it minimizes risk taking for a long time.

> *In an innovative culture, you must learn to live*
> *with failure, but never to accept it!*
> Dr. Geoff Nicholson
> 3M Vice President,
> International R&D

Environment

The category I've labeled environment is the sum of the six must-do topics I've just discussed. Added together, they provide the desired environment for innovators to produce creative ideas and products. This environment is free of barriers and celebrates challenge and risk taking. The innovative organization gets a thrill from exploring the unknown. Here's a list of some of the ingredients found in an innovative environment:

- Individual freedom

- Openness to risk and tolerance for failure

- Management avoidance of wrong signals, such as those listed on page 16

- Employment stability
- Reward and recognition programs
- Hiring enterprising people
- Sharing information and crossfertilization
- Empowering and trusting employees

First come the expectation, challenge, and resources to innovate. The more information and experience available, the more likely innovation will occur. Remove barriers to communication. Share information not only internally, but also with customers. When your goal is to develop new products, customer interactions should be joint efforts with sales and/or marketing personnel. Encourage technical employees to spend some time in the customer's workplace, observing the general work flow and even competitive products. Providing this kind of knowledge for laboratory employees is the first step in finding and developing product ideas that are one step ahead of competition and which satisfy customer needs— even some needs the customer may not yet be aware of.

If I am building a mountain and stop before the
last basket of earth is placed on the summit, I have failed.
Confucius

II.

BUILDING THE CULTURE
FOR INNOVATION

PERHAPS THE BIGGEST CHALLENGE in business today is avoiding torpid bureaucracy, in which form takes precedence over substance and an inverse relationship exists between effort and effect. On the one hand, 3M traditionally has done this by decentralizing into small, autonomous business units that can concentrate on new ideas and enterprises. On the other hand, business realities today often require a consolidation of effort with large customers who buy many products. For example, a vast retail chain may prefer to deal with a single 3M point of contact, instead of 15 or 20 small units. The goal thus becomes to retain the advantages of smallness within the structure while achieving critical mass elsewhere—as determined by customer needs and requirements. To do this successfully requires a high level of flexibility and a willingness to adapt even that which presently is a source of innovation and success. It also requires an extremely high level of coordination among business units and functions such as laboratory, marketing, distribution, and even accounting.

Today, neither big nor small is beautiful or bad. The correct answer is: "It all depends."

Whether we approach customers on a macro or micro scale, one thing is constant. Within our structure, we organize to work small, either by establishing tiny business units or by forming truly independent teams within larger organizations. In either case, the unit or team can concentrate on its own idea, technology, or product. This approach helps us to achieve the seemingly contradictory goals of being large and small simultaneously. Empowerment permits this approach; a controlling management would choke the life out of it.

Strategies

A company's strategies should drive innovation continuously and pervasively. The 3M Innovation Wheel, shown in Figure 2, summarizes the strategies at 3M that do this. These strategies are permanent and continue much as they have in the past, regardless of business or laboratory location. Company managers frequently communicate them to employees and outsiders at functions, meetings, and informal gatherings. Communicating company strategies consistently is one of the most effective methods of transmitting a clear, constant message to employees about the value of innovation and its role in corporate growth. A sampling of permanent strategies follows.

Financial

- Ten percent annual growth in both sales and earnings

- Thirty percent of total sales must come from new products introduced to the market in the last four years

- Ten percent of total sales must come from new products introduced during the calendar year

All Employees

- The strategy of finding new jobs for employees involved with failed projects sends employees an emphatic message that risk taking truly is all right.

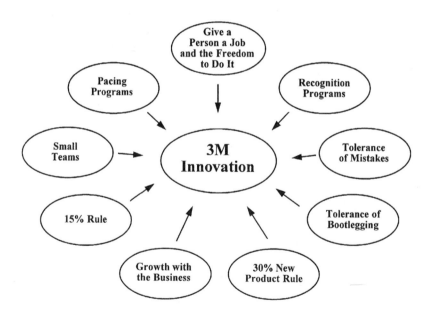

Figure 2.   3M innovation wheel (© 3M)

- A stable employment record results in lower turnover in personnel, which translates into consistent extension of businesses and, occasionally, dramatic improvement in market position.

Technical Employees

- All technical personnel have 15% of their regular work time to devote to ideas of their own choosing.

- Technical personnel are encouraged to visit customer sites, which gives them a strong dose of marketplace reality and exposes them to customer ideas and needs.

- Forming R&D organizations of laboratory heads (Technical Council), laboratory employees (Technical Forum), groups focusing on core technologies (Technical Forum Chapters/Technology Centers), or key senior scientists (Corporate Scientists Council) promotes the use and sharing of technologies and new product breakthroughs in the company.

- A dual-ladder promotional system allows technical people to be rewarded on an equal basis, whether their contributions come at the bench or in management.

- All technologies belong to the entire company and as a result are available for anyone in the company to use.

The last point deserves further explanation, since it is one of 3M's hidden keys of success. Sharing technology is a critical element in innovation. Sharing avoids reinvention of the wheel, and thus facilitates process improvements and the commercialization of new products. In most cases, these new products involve more than one technology.

3M technologies are shared around 3M's world—literally. Most of our laboratories are at corporate headquarters in St. Paul. However, we have significant technical operations in Austin, Texas, and throughout Europe, Latin America, and the Pacific Rim nations. Strong and continuing efforts are made to keep all of these technical organizations "in the loop" and to transfer advances in one region to produce additional new products elsewhere.

Entrepreneurship and Product Champions

One of 3M's most famous product lines, Scotch™ tape, was invented in 1930. This fact is important because, not only has this product line been highly successful for many years, but the process used in developing it has become a keystone in the foundation that supports 3M's culture of innovation. This process is institutionalized in 3M, yet it still is not easy to describe. Here's a try at it: The 3M innovation culture globally promotes a system of supportive management, entrepreneurship, and encouragement for product champions. This environment is promoted in all operations, regardless of where they are located. The central idea is that the 3M organizational environment has helped the company succeed and it consists of the things already noted.

New products—such as Post-it Notes—are important, but only half of the 3M innovation story. The other half consists of continuously reinventing existing product lines to maximize their useful lifetime in the market. That's because *today's* product lines generate the financial resources we need to commercialize *tomorrow's* products.

The mark of highest originality lies in the ability to develop a familiar idea so fruitfully that it would seem no one else would ever have discovered so much to be hidden in it.

Goethe

Here are some management practices that allow organizations, regardless of size, to maintain a culture of entrepreneurship.

- All employees, but especially the technical employees, are encouraged to be creative and develop their own ideas in an environment of innovation.

- Failure is an accepted and essential part of progress.

- The atmosphere is open and informal.

- Company growth comes from both innovative new products and evolutionary spin-offs.

- New products and processes have measurable targets.

- New ideas and innovations are shared worldwide.

The following management practices work specifically for technical organizations:

- All employees have access to a highly diversified technology base and are encouraged to make full use of it.

- The company combines multiple technology plat-
forms to produce unique products (synergy).

- Technology exchange among technical personnel and
among laboratories is open and free.

- Employees, especially laboratory employees, are from
different cultures.

Organization Objectives and Targets

Stretch Targets

3M's vision of being the most innovative enterprise
in the world and the preferred supplier in the markets it
serves is a *stretch target*. Organizations that aim for the top
know that the only way to get there is by maintaining current activities through incremental innovations while constantly supporting attempts to fundamentally change the
way things are done. Stretch targets force the organization
to change and adopt new ways to meet its ambitious targets that doing things the old way cannot. Organizations
that set comfortable goals within easy reach become resis-
tant to change, and the dominos begin falling. First, innovation slows down and may even cease. If that happens,
you become a low-calorie lunch for hungry competitors.

To grow, organizations must continuously improve
what they do and create new products or processes. This
approach is simple, but very difficult to execute in organizations that lack an innovative culture. In noninnovative
organizations, tension builds up between forces that seek

to keep things the same and forces that seek change. Without innovation, this tension becomes unbalanced toward the status quo. The need to change (new products and processes) is neglected, and that spells trouble for the future. Issues of incremental and fundamental growth both need to be addressed.

3M's primary growth strategy is to sell more existing products into new markets and to sell new products into new or existing markets. An overall sales-growth goal— with a large new-product component—ensures that both strategic elements receive the proper attention.

For decades, 3M businesses were challenged to produce 25% of their sales from products that were new within the previous five years. This requirement helped to stimulate product development. It also taught managers that the long-term health of the company was as important as current results.

Since 1993, the new-product sales component target has been raised to a *30% rule*. Now the target is that 30% of the sales from each business unit should come from new products introduced in the last four years. Raising the hurdle means that the organization must find ways to speed up. By continuously increasing our new-product goal, 3M sends a clear message that no business unit can rest on its laurels, no matter how good its results.

Pacing Programs

The global recession of the early 1990s triggered the creation of another 3M strategy to accelerate sales growth. The company established a portfolio of initiatives it calls *Pacing Programs.*

"MOVE 'EM OUT !"

Figure 3.   Stretch targets enhance innovation (© 3M)

Pacing Programs are special growth opportunities that have the potential to change the basis of competition in a market, the way 3M™ VHB™ (very high bond) tapes replace spot welding and rivets in many industrial applications. Another: Our 3M™ Scotch-Brite™ Never-Rust Wool Soap Pads are made out of recycled plastic bottles and outperform steel wool without rusting or splintering. They are the first major innovation in the steel wool market in

75 years and became a market leader within one year of their introduction.

Every 3M business unit is expected to identify two to four Pacing Programs, and we normally have a corporate portfolio of about 200. Many are new-product programs, but others include major advances in process innovation, unit-cost reduction, and even marketing initiatives and logistics/service excellence. 3M front-loads these programs with additional money and people, so they can contribute as quickly as possible.

The Pacing Program strategy is viewed as a means to achieve the company's financial goals, even during slow-growth economic periods. Financial goals are really numerical ways of expressing how well 3M is answering these types of questions:

- Are we the leaders in our markets?

- Are we creating opportunities for our employees?

- Do we have the confidence of our investors?

All of these important questions relate to some aspect of the way 3M has built and maintains its culture of innovation.

III.

Maintaining an Innovative Culture

P OST-IT NOTES EXEMPLIFY 3M'S ability to combine
and extend technologies and also to overcome
unexpected problems imaginatively.

The Post-it story begins in 1964 with a *Polymers for Adhesives* program in the company's Central Research Laboratories. 3M scientist Spencer Silver tested a new monomer by overloading a reaction mixture far beyond textbook standards, to see what would happen. He discovered a novel substance that clung to its own molecules better than to other molecules; it *tacked* between two surfaces but wouldn't bond firmly to either. It also was outside the scope of 3M's research into ever-stronger adhesives.

The adhesive was looked upon as an interesting novelty, and it even was used to create a no-pin bulletin board. The product was not successful, and interest waned in Silver's invention.

In the 3M tradition, Silver tenaciously promoted his adhesive around the company. Applications and support were not forthcoming, but at least the adhesive became well known in 3M's technical community. The *Eureka moment* finally occurred in 1974 when another scientist, Art Fry, decided to play with the adhesive. Fry sang in a church choir, and he wanted to create a hymnal marker that wouldn't fall out of the book, but could be removed without tearing pages. After several experiments, he came up with just what he wanted, as well as an insight that led

" I FOUND ONE THAT REALLY STICKS THIS TIME!"

Figure 4. Focus on the objective,
but expect the unexpected (© 3M)

Silver and Fry to look for innovative ways to use this interesting material on other kinds of paper.

Very quickly, a number of other 3M scientists became involved, along with division technical director Geoff Nicholson and general manager Joseph Ramey. Process development and design refinements followed, with Art Fry building prototype manufacturing hardware at home to demonstrate that it *was possible* to coat adhesive onto roll-stock paper and process it into pads. (Fry had to knock out a basement wall in his home to be able to move the hardware to his 3M lab.)

The nature of hurdles to overcome switched from technical to sales. The Post-it program was at the point of cancellation in an early test market, because of a near-zero response. Ramey and Nicholson visited one of the test cities, Richmond, Virginia. They discovered that people didn't respond, because they had never used anything like the repositionable notes. This led to a last-chance market-ing test—the *Boise Blitz* in Idaho. The division flooded Boise with sales representatives demonstrating product and handing out samples in banks, offices, stores—everywhere paper clips and staplers might be used. Sparks were struck, and demand ignited.

Post-it Notes were introduced nationally following that success and have grown into a family of products in pervasive use around the world. Post-it products now are offered in many standard versions, plus special shapes for file-folder tabs, phone messages, document-routing slips and "to do" lists. Other Post-it products include tape flags, glue sticks, and a removable version of 3M™ Magic™

Transparent Tape. Easel-sized Post-it pads are newly available for brainstorming sessions and formal meetings. They affix to walls without tape and won't damage wallpaper, paint, or wood surfaces.

Everyone Is an Innovator

Ideas are the lifeblood of an innovative organization. On the other hand, not all of the people in any organization are born with the natural talent to think creatively—or to ask questions that promote discussions, new concepts, or theories. Unfortunately, many organizations don't recognize this fact. All organizations need to be taught and given the tools to feel comfortable in creating new paradigms. An innovative organization is obliged to provide the resources all employees need to become creative thinkers. The attitude should be that every process or operation in the organization requires constant improvement. Once such an attitude is entrenched, the result is a continuous flow of innovative suggestions for improvement.

> *To win you have to risk loss.*
> Jean-Claude Killy

Innovation is not limited to technology generation and new-product development activities in the laboratory. Every function and employee in an organization should work under the expectation that they will be creative. If something can be improved or done better, do it. At the end of every activity, hold a review session to decide how to do it better the next time.

For consideration here, however, comments will be focused on activities and expectations involving laboratories and technical employees.

Tools

Idea generation is the first step in the new-product generation and development process. The primary thing to remember is that a continuous flow of quality new products from a laboratory does not just happen. It is a planned process, and the tools available for establishing and enhancing the process are many and readily available. A partial listing of tools for generating ideas includes:

- Customer needs identification (articulated and unarticulated)

- Focus panels

- Facilitated and focused brainstorming

- Poster Sessions and mini-technology trade shows

- Suggestion boxes and idea banks

- Courses and books on enhancing creativity and innovation

    Let's look at each of these tools in a little more detail.

Customer Needs Identification

Customers are one of the best and most logical sources of new-product ideas and features. Customer input is the compass used to guide both the ideational process and the new product design and development process. This source of information has been recognized almost from the beginning of time. However, only in recent times has industry researched and developed formal methods for obtaining customer input at the dawn of development—when fundamental changes can be made.

In years past, the strategy of "make-a-little-sell-a-little" did incorporate customer input, but was primarily an evolutionary tool that was used to modify new generations of the same product. These, in effect, were small bets, which innovative companies still need to make. However, along with small bets, companies also must fund a set of big opportunities (e.g., Pacing Programs) with huge sales potential. And this is why it's important to get customers involved with development all the way from the concept phase right through to test marketing.

Accurate and detailed customer input greatly influences the final success or failure of product in today's marketplace. This is why it is important for technical people to visit customers with sales and marketing people. They need to find out, first hand, about work flow and how people use existing products, including those of competitors. This approach not only enhances the innovation process in the laboratory, but it also increases the likelihood of generating ideas that will be commercially successful.

Understanding customer operations and needs is the first step in providing innovative solutions for market needs. In preparation for customer visits, employees should have some training in listening to what the customer actually is telling them when they describe their product needs and preferences. The researcher, salesperson, or technical service representative can easily misinterpret the terms the customer uses.

For example, a customer said that a competitive product was preferable because "it was more solid." By watching people use the product and asking several knowledgeable questions, a researcher discovered that "more solid" meant that the competitive product "clicked" when the attachment was made, giving the "more solid" feeling. Designers were then able to incorporate this same solid feeling into the product, eliminating an advantage in perception for the competitive product.

Experience teaches that there are two types of customer needs. One type can be clearly articulated by the customer. The other type is unarticulated, or not obvious to the customer. Filling your customers' articulated needs may constantly reinforce your sales base, but successfully fulfilling unarticulated needs has the potential to lead to major new businesses. Today, consulting firms specialize in helping organizations define both the recognized and unrecognized needs of their customers.

Focus Panels

Focus panels, using potential customers as panel members, are an extremely useful tool. Once potential products have been shown to be technically feasible, having a customer focus panel look at the product provides good insurance that development is moving in the right direction. Customer input on features or deficiencies is a strong motivator for laboratory members to enhance innovation.

Facilitated and Focused Brainstorming

Building a family of products in a defined market area is a task that lends itself well to the use of facilitated and focused brainstorming sessions. Brainstorming has been used for many years and still has its place in enhancing innovation today. Six or eight creative individuals work with an unbiased facilitator to generate a large number of ideas for potential new products in a short period of time.

This process is most effective when the market area is well defined and the process is focused on a specific aspect of that market. A typical example might be a session focused on the interior lighting of an automobile. The market is the automotive market, the focus is on the specific opportunity of interior lighting and what can be done with it to make significant improvements that satisfy customer needs.

In order to have an open and freewheeling idea session, remember that all ideas are worthwhile. Encourage participants not to judge each other's ideas, but to explore the full range of ideas as a team. Make sure that every contributor gets credit for every idea. The process for doing this is simple. Give every participant a notepad on which to write ideas before presenting them. Post-it Notes are excellent for this process, since each idea can be recorded along with the name of the person submitting the idea. Post these ideas on a wall and group them according to subject. As ideas are presented, the product focus is refined until one idea stands out from the others. Brainstorming can continue to determine features, advantages, and benefits. When the session is over, provide each participant with a written summary of the brainstorming session's findings. This is helpful if an additional session is to be held, or if the brainstorming process has progressed far enough for a laboratory feasibility study.

Poster Sessions and Mini-Technology Trade Shows

For companies that own diverse technologies and product lines, poster sessions can be a helpful way to stimulate technology transfer. At 3M, a three-day Technical Forum event every year gives technical and marketing people a chance to learn about technologies and products developed in other parts of our decentralized company. Technology special-interest groups stage other, smaller-scale sessions throughout the year. These poster sessions continue to prove their value in helping researchers discover ideas and technologies that they can leverage into their own businesses.

Suggestion Boxes and Idea Banks

The concept of the suggestion box is nearly as old as American business. Yet it remains an important source of ideas for the innovative organization. Employees record their ideas for new products, improving work procedures, cost reductions, and so on, and submit them electronically or on paper for management to consider. This tool is successful when employees know that they are expected to submit ideas and that something will be done with the ideas.

There are two fundamental principles to processing idea submissions. First, management must evaluate every idea submitted and respond to the person who submitted the idea. Second, no idea is bad, so any idea not acted on should go into an "idea file." The ideas in this file should be reviewed periodically for possible acceptance, even if they need to be combined with other ideas that have been submitted. It is not uncommon in a laboratory of 100 people to have several thousand ideas in its idea bank at any given time. Even such large numbers should be reconsidered once or twice a year. Forget to acknowledge ideas, or discard them precipitously, and the flow of new ideas will slow to a trickle and perhaps dry up altogether.

It's also important to avoid a "not-invented-here" syndrome, because 3M can't be all things to everybody in technology. To remain state-of-the-art, the company invests in about 40 venture capital funds at any given time. In turn, these funds invest in more than a thousand companies.

This gives us an important window into the world of new technologies. In addition at 3M:

- We attend industry seminars and trade shows.

- We read about new technologies in journals.

- We scan data bases.

- We respond to direct inquiries from the public, which number between 150 and 200 per month.

In recent years, we've also held several technology exchange programs at 3M Center. Each time, we have invited 40 to 50 companies to bring their technologies to a 3M audience of about 2,000 3M technical and marketing people. We also establish venture agreements and vendor relationships. And our executives sometimes sit on small-company advisory boards.

Courses and Books on Enhancing Creativity and Innovation

Courses and consulting firms can help companies enhance creativity and innovation. These courses and firms offer a uniform approach to improving the creativity of the organization by concentrating on improving the ability of individuals to innovate.

While it is not possible to "create an Edison" through courses, seminars, and individual study, it is possible to enhance an individual's creative and innovative skills considerably.

Books can provide considerable insight into methodologies useful for enhancing the creativity and innovative ability of researchers, technicians, or marketers. Here are some thoughts about a few of the books that discuss innovation:

- James M. Higgin's *101 Creative Problem Solving Techniques: The Handbook of New Ideas for Business* provides a wealth of suggestions on how to get started in enhancing individual creativity and innovation. Two additional books by Higgins are *Innovate or Evaporate: The Profile of the Innovative Organization* and *Escape From the Maze: Increasing Personal and Group Creativity Potential.*

- *Profiting From Innovation,* by W. C. Howard, Jr. and B. R. Guile, suggests how management can enhance innovation in American laboratories. This book focuses primarily on "getting more managers, executives, and other key individuals—both in and out of government—to learn, feel, understand, and appreciate how technological innovation is spawned, nurtured, financed, and managed into new technological businesses that grow, provide jobs, and satisfy people."

- Michalak's *Thinkertoys* offers approaches designed to help individuals come up with unique ideas.

- Zangwill's *Lightning Strategies for Innovation* shows how companies create new business opportunities.

These books are only a few of many that provide considerable insight into methodologies used for enhancing the creativity and innovative ability of researchers, technicians, or marketers. In addition, a quick literature search for articles on innovation, published in just the last five years, can yield dozens of excellent references.

> *The only means of strengthening one's intellect is to make up one's mind about nothing—to let the mind be a thoroughfare for all thoughts.*
>
> John Keats

IV.

Reward and Honor the Heroes

O NE OF THE GREATEST motivations for innovation is the expectation that the organization will recognize and honor outstanding work. 3M focuses most of its award and recognition programs on new products and innovation, because this reinforces the 3M vision, which is "to be recognized as the most innovative enterprise in the world." Thus, emphasizing new products and innovation is just one more step in enhancing and promoting creativity. How better to get the message across that "innovation is the way to succeed around here?"

Recognition can be formal or informal, and both are necessary.

Formal recognition by senior management is the most effective mechanism for rewarding and honoring those responsible for innovation and creativity. All such efforts need to be well planned and scrupulously fair, or the stature of the recognition will suffer. When it comes to recognizing innovation, it's better to do nothing than to do it wrong.

"SIMON, HERE, IS OUR TOP INNOVATOR."

Figure 5.   Reward innovators (© 3M)

While formal programs are important, they're bolstered by informal forms of recognition. These include a working atmosphere where management values good work and recognizes it on a daily basis.

In the innovative organization, compensation must reward outstanding individual performance as well as managerial responsibilities. It can be disastrous to innovation if technical people see only one way to advance—into management. (It's especially tragic when an outstanding scientist becomes a mediocre manager just to advance in pay.) At 3M, we handle this dichotomy through a dual-ladder pay system that establishes parallel promotional paths for technical workers and managers. It's possible for a research scientist at 3M to advance to the rank of Corporate Scientist, equivalent to director, without leaving the bench. (The dual ladder also exists for 3M sales representatives, who can become Account Executives, which are equivalent to sale managers.) This approach allows employees maximum flexibility in planning their careers, with many moving back and forth between bench and management sides of the dual ladder.

Several corporate recognition programs at 3M, described below, illustrate how the process can be made to work. In addition, many individual business units have their own recognition programs as well.

3M Corporate Award and Recognition Programs

- Golden Step Award
- Carlton Society
- Technical Circle of Excellence
- Patent Plaques
- Genesis Program

Golden Step Award

The Golden Step Award recognizes cross-functional teams that bring high quality new products to the marketplace.

New-product programs are nominated by the business unit heads and selected by a corporate committee after the product reaches a goal for profitable sales on a global basis. After nomination, the product has three years in which to reach the sales figure and attain profitability. Annually about half of the eligible programs receive the award. The selection is based on the uniqueness and quality of the product. Awardees are honored at a formal banquet attended by all winning team members, their guests, and top management.

Carlton Society

The Carlton Society is an honorary organization of individuals who have made important contributions to the progress of 3M's science and technology. It is named for R. P. Carlton, 3M's first head of research and fifth president. The purpose of the society is to stimulate and encourage technical employees to excel in their scientific and technological work. This award recognizes the longer-term contributions of technical personnel. Nominations are made on an annual basis by peers and selection is made by all members of the 3M Technical Council (laboratory heads of the larger laboratories) and the Corporate Scientists (top scientific level at 3M).

Recognition is given at a special meeting where all technical personnel are invited. Awards are presented by the senior vice president of research and development and the CEO. There is an annual reception and banquet for all Carlton Society members and their guests. Each new member of the society is given a small bust of Mr. Carlton engraved with recipient's name and date of election to membership in the society. Almost 150 members have been elected to the Carlton Society since the beginning of 3M.

Technical Circle of Excellence

The Technical Circle of Excellence program was implemented in 1982 with the objective of recognizing excellence in the laboratory during a one-year time frame. The focus is on younger technical employees, support personnel, and team leaders or champions. Awardees are nominated by peers and selected by peer selection committees. Nomination and selection criteria are based on performance above and beyond assigned tasks.

Each laboratory is allotted one or more awardees, depending on laboratory size, in each of three categories: technical excellence, support excellence, and championing or team-leading excellence. Large laboratories (100 or more personnel) would have one awardee in the championing or team category, one in the support category, and three in the technical category. Smaller laboratories would have only one awardee in each category, while medium-sized laboratories would have two awardees in the technical category and one in each of the other categories.

All laboratory awardees and their spouses or guests are entertained by senior management at a reception and banquet where 15 to 20 corporate awardees are announced—the "best-of-the-best." The corporate awardees are selected by peer groups before the banquet and are evenly distributed by major business area (sectors), corporate research, and international laboratories. Each awardee receives a gold ring to commemorate his or her achievement and is treated to a weekend with spouse or guest at a company conference facility.

Patent Plaques

Each person named on an issued 3M patent receives a plaque that shows a replica of the patent. Those who receive 20 or more patents have the choice of receiving a separate plaque for each patent or a brass name plate for each patent that hangs from a master plaque. Plaques are presented by laboratory heads at a suitable laboratory function.

Genesis Program

The Genesis Program was implemented in 1984 to provide a mechanism for encouraging and funding good, new-product or new-technology ideas that were not being pursued. Through this program, 3M researchers are encouraged to focus some of their innovative abilities on generating ideas that do not fit the strategic needs or directions of the laboratory or business unit to which they belong. Company management annually sets aside a small pool of money to distribute as Genesis grants. A review committee consisting of three or four laboratory heads and three or four senior scientists manages the process and selects ideas for funding. Winners of Genesis grants use them to pursue the ideas that they feel have good potential, but are outside the market focus of their operation.

The company thinks that some of these ideas might result in new products having characteristics that could create entirely new businesses.

Individuals or teams that submit ideas selected for Genesis funding receive $50,000 to $90,000 depending on need, for one year during which the objective is to prove the feasibility of the idea. A second year of funding at a level up to $100,000 is possible for ideas that show significant potential. In addition to the funds, a requisition for a technician or support person is also provided to the grant winners. This enables the project to be managed using "15% rule" time. Thus, employees can also continue to accomplish their regularly assigned tasks.

The Genesis Program not only has produced commercially successful new products, but also many U.S. and foreign patents and technical papers. In addition, Genesis has been an effective morale builder for the entire technical community.

Recommendations

Here are a few recommendations to consider when establishing organizational reward and recognition strategies.

- Use your vision and strategic business plan to set the goals for your organization's innovation, recognition and reward program.

- Structure formal recognition and reward programs to ensure that every employee has an opportunity to win.

- Celebrate individual and team achievements with form al recognition programs.

Given the right working environment, most innovators excel because they're internally motivated—not because of the cash value of a potential award. Focus formal recognition programs on a celebration of outstanding individual or team contributions as judged by an employee's peers.

V.

THE ROLE OF TEAMS

THE CARTOON SHOWS A GROUP of businesspeople sailing by the Statue of Liberty, looking up at its message: "Give us your teaming masses, yearning to be free."

The image is good for a chuckle, but it also concentrates our attention on why teams are so important in our time-compressed world, where Monday's innovations can wither into Tuesday's trivialities.

Team Performance

Freedom definitely is one of the reasons for the importance of teams, and flexibility is another. Together, freedom and flexibility add up to performance. Teams provide both.

Freedom

In a team structure, members have this freedom to do what needs to be done to accomplish the team's purpose. They are not constrained by the standardized procedures of functional bureaucrats. Goal-oriented, multidisciplinary teams operate with an alertness and suppleness impossible in organizations hidebound by a layered hierarchy struggling to coordinate and control myriad disconnected functions.

These functions usually are depicted as silos or smokestacks and operate according to the old paradigm of "throwing the new design over the wall," from one functional group to the next.

While silo and smokestack organizations operate in sequence, cross-functional teams perform in parallel. Jobs that traditionally were done as separate disciplines in the laboratory, manufacturing, accounting, purchasing, and marketing are now done simultaneously by multifunctional teams.

Chrysler is the obvious example of the advantage of a team-oriented approach. Recognizing the need to accelerate change, the automaker reorganized into three multifunctional platform teams:

- Trucks and vans

- Large cars

- Small cars

These platform teams include not only scientists and engineers, but also marketing people, financial analysts, and factory workers. The platform-team concept helped Chrysler slash a year from the development time for its LH family of mid-size sedans, producing these cars in the world class time of 39 months, with half the people and at half the cost of a conventional design program.

In the process, Chrysler not only moved back from the edge of extinction; it leapfrogged the abyss to set the U.S. standard for auto design and development.

Flexibility

Flexibility is as important as freedom to team-building. Teams can go outside the organization to include companies with which the organization has built business partnerships, or suppliers who can provide unique resources to speed development and lower R&D costs. Customers, too, may become team members, either directly or indirectly, through focus groups and other research.

Cooperation between 3M's data storage products business and computer drive manufacturers offers a textbook example of a symbiotic relationship. 3M produces new, higher capacity data cartridges on which to store computer programs and files. Drive manufacturers produce the hardware on which these new, high capacity cartridges work. 3M cartridges are unusable without these advanced drives—and vice versa.

As a result, data cartridge systems advanced from a storage capacity of 128 megabytes to 1.6 gigabytes. This storage capacity is equal to 800 3.5-inch computer diskettes—up from 64 diskettes—and in less than a decade. The newest cartridge/drive system is backward compatible with earlier generations.

This means all older, lower-capacity data cartridges can be accessed from the new drives. Customers benefit, because they can use the latest high-capacity storage system without having to transfer previously stored information to the new format.

Empowered Teams

However a team is composed, all members work toward the team goal, not just on performing their individual tasks. Thus, emphasis is on producing a marketable product ASAP, not taking things one step at a time, from idea to laboratory, to manufacturing and—at long-delayed last—to market. In the team paradigm, teams gain points only for completing the jigsaw puzzle, not for producing the pieces.

Empowered teams are closest to the business action and, thus, are best qualified to make business decisions. As a result, they need not be managed closely and have decisions made for them. This serves to strip away the need for sedimentary layers of supervision that build up over time, slowing progress to a geological pace. With empowered teams, a large organization need not become ponderous and slower with growth and age.

My experience with teams has been in the area of product development. However, teams can be employed successfully anywhere an organization can gather a real-time combination of skills, experiences, and abilities to focus on a special need.

For example, seven 3M divisions have formed an Industrial Markets program to provide customers with one-stop shopping for sales, service, and technical support for a wide range of products. In the past, customers worked individually with these seven divisions.

Employees in other business areas organized teams to concentrate on their own market areas. Two such team efforts are in the areas of consumer products and office products. They draw products from throughout 3M to meet customer needs without the battles over turf common to silo- and smokestack-oriented organizations.

One 3M division is organized into business development units, each containing three to four teams. Another unit is organized so that its customer contacts go far beyond the conventional relationship between their sales representative and the customer's purchasing agent.

In this organization, our shipping people work directly with the customer's receiving people. Their ordering department directly contacts our receiving organization.

When the customer's computer expert, "Fred," talks to our computer expert, "Mary," it's on a first-name basis that enhances problem solving. Since neither is an abstraction to the other, they tend not to let organizational barriers get in the way of problem solving.

In any situation, the combined expertise of several individuals working together as a team invariably produces significantly better results than the same individuals working alone and independently. In an innovative culture, teams work hand in hand to bring "best practices" and accelerate the time it takes to turn an idea into a technology and a technology into a new product in the marketplace.

Because teams focus on one goal, they respond to stretch challenges that energize them to achieve extraordinary contributions. An outstanding example of team vision is President Kennedy's challenge to America: Be first to put a man on the moon. The results are history, but the lessons are repeated daily.

3M has been using teams for more than three decades. In the early years, the company's teams were used primarily for product development and, of necessity, were small—usually only five or six members. Today, 3M teams are larger and truly cross-functional, but still contain the basic core team of five or six people.

A core team consists of members from the laboratory, marketing, manufacturing, quality, and the controller's organization. The leader of a product team is usually from the laboratory. However, leadership may—or may not—move to someone from marketing or manufacturing as the program moves through the phases of development. Subteam members can range from advertising and public relations to human resources, and from logistics to law.

Cross-Functional Teams

The formation of a 3M cross-functional team is standard and probably similar to what most industrial firms use. However, at 3M the management sponsor and functional resource manager are critically important to the success of teams. Fortunately, their roles are easily defined.

The Role of Management Sponsor

- Assure management understanding, consensus, and the buy-in needed to support the effort.

- Address barriers that impede progress:
  - Priorities
  - Conflict resolution
  - Resources, including technology, equipment, etc.
  - Funding for the role of team leader
- Clarify project objectives and priorities.
- Assure that team roles are identified and communicated.
- Establish operating principles up front (ground rules, boundaries, etc.)
- Maintain focus on key issues.
- Assure conflict resolution and overcome barriers.
- Monitor progress against the plan and adjust as required.
- Manage the budget, resources, and the schedule.
- Report project status to the management support team.
- Initiate team recognition of the role of each team member.
- Provide functional department expertise, and coordinate functional activities, communications, and budgets.
- Innovate and contribute ideas.
- Help resolve conflicts and overcome barriers.

- Recommend solutions.

- Help implement solutions.

- Identify and validate continually with customers their expectations and importance.

- Develop a mix of product and service target requirements that maximize overall customer satisfaction.

The Role of Functional Resource Manager

- Guide the business unit through the commercialization improvement process.

- Act as a change agent to establish business unit buy-in.

- Support the team leader.

- Provide continuous improvement of the functional process.

The main differences in the way 3M uses the team and what we have seen in other organizations lie primarily in the *power* given to the team and the team leader. Team members submit a plan for management review. With plan approval comes the complete support and trust of management. The team is given the resources necessary to complete the program and the freedom to act on the plan. From this point forward, second-guessing is out.

The team has full control of its program, but is expected to deliver the product to the market and on schedule. Progress is reviewed periodically during the development program by business unit management.

If the program succeeds, the success is celebrated.

If the program fails, the company considers it a learning process that is dissected to learn what went wrong and how other teams can avoid any problems discovered.

Special-Purpose Teams

3M uses special purpose teams that capitalize on the strengths of teams rather than on diverse, fragmented, individual efforts. This approach can be illustrated by the way the 3M technical community enhances the overall productivity of laboratories in their new product development efforts. Examples of such special-purpose teams would be:

- Time-compression teams

- Formalized decision-making teams

- Customer-need identification teams

- Quality improvement teams

- Cost reduction teams

- Technical audit teams

Each special purpose team is different. The focus is different. The method of operation is different. The personnel assigned and the home department of the personnel are quite different. The overall objective, however, is the same—bring the collective expertise and skills of a group of highly diverse individuals together to focus on solving a specific problem or set of problems. For example, in the area of reducing time to market, the team consisted of 25 members, each representing a subteam that was highly skilled in a best practice and capable of transferring that expertise to members of a cross-functional, new-product, development team. Examples of such best practices or subteams are:

- Project planning

- QFD (customer requirements)

- Simultaneous global market introduction

- Agency approvals (FDA, UL, etc.)

- Patenting and trademarks

- Design for manufacture

- Packaging

- Cost reduction

Each subteam is a highly responsive unit that is available to work with any developmental team anywhere in the company, at the request of the team leader. They transfer the experience and knowledge gained from years of collective new-product development experience that can help make developmental programs progress more smoothly and, thus, shorten the time to market.

Experience shows that if the strategic thinking associated with the front-end project planning is very thorough; the required technology is well in hand; the product design is frozen early; and the available best practices are used where appropriate; a minimum of 50% reduction in time to market can be achieved.

The "teaming masses, yearning to be free" are now ready to move to the truly boundaryless organization, operating with a culture and structure that draws talent and resources from wherever and however that are required to do any job faster and more effectively.

VI.

CONCLUSIONS

E STABLISHING OR ENHANCING AN innovative culture requires considerable planning, commitment, and follow-through on the part of all management employees. Establishing a workforce that continually adapts to change requires considerable time to build the proper culture and then constant attention to maintain the culture, but is well worth the effort. Once people are committed, the results can be truly outstanding.

Getting employees to be self-confident, self-motivated, and goal-oriented, however, requires that management itself be creative and expend a lot of energy. It takes as much management effort to nurture an innovative culture as it does to control faceless masses or risk-aversive drones.

The following list of "keys to innovative new products" provides a compact summary of 3M's culture and a how-to list for establishing or enhancing a viable, innovative culture in any organization.

- New-product culture.

- New-product expectation is 30% of sales in four years.

- Top managers are "patient, new-product bankers."

- New products are needs/technology driven.

- New-product ideas come from everywhere.

- Resources are available for good ideas.

- Everyone is expected to be an innovator.

- New-product champions are heroes.

- Many diverse technologies are available to researchers.

- All technologies are available to all technical employees for use in their innovations, free of charge.

- Best ideas, technologies, and practices are shared.

- Well-defined new-product introduction system is in place.

- Many experts are available.

- Bootlegging/boundary-crossing is accepted and made easy.

- Many recognition/reward systems are in place.

Measuring the Success of Innovation Programs and Efforts

A wide variety of actions have been listed for enhancing and implementing innovative practices in organizations, but how do you measure your success? Measurements have been developed to measure the number of ideas generated; the number of problems solved; the number of patents; the number of new products; the number of new businesses generated or entered; the percent increase in sales and profits, and much more. The key is to create yardsticks that reflect the output measured. Do not try to compare one business with another. The market opportunities are different. The people and the strategic approach are different. Investment levels are different. Instead, focus on year-to-year improvement within a unit.

Achieving the goals that result from formulating a solid strategy is a good indicator of success. At 3M, an annual innovation goal is to have 30% of worldwide sales come from products introduced to the market in the last four years. For companies, sales and income for each business should grow at least as fast as competitors. As your efforts to build the innovative environment continue, expect to outperform the competition. In a government setting, productivity should increase year by year.

Use of rigorous measuring techniques always raises the question of whether or not they will destroy innovation. Measuring what you are looking for will not hinder innovation if you use the measurements wisely. Do not restrict the idea process. Chaos is an essential part of innovation. Let the front end of the process be unstructured and very informal—even different for each part of the organization, if necessary. Begin using metrics only after a consensus exists for what is important to measure. Earlier, the concept of strategies that drive innovation was discussed. The goals that come from creating strategy contain measurements. These measurements should be applied and then reported to everyone. The organization learns through repeated communications that the reported results are significant. Be aware that timing also is important. For example, don't begin measuring a new-product program until a decision has been made to go ahead with it. After beginning the project, measure to reinforce the urgency of successfully completing the program's goals.

A word of caution. Organizations typically achieve the metrics they set for themselves. You need to know what's important to measure. For example, do you want to measure against a goal of delivering a new product to market in half the time? That's a good idea, but it assumes—perhaps wrongly—that the new product will meet customer expectations. What you really want to measure is whether the product satisfies the customer and he or she has received it as quickly as possible. It is without value to deliver in half the time a product nobody wants to buy.

In the final analysis, the true indication of how successfully an organization has created or changed its level of innovation is reflected in the performance of the organization as a whole. Has the organization been revitalized? Have sales and profits improved according to expectations? Has the morale of the employees improved? Has the outlook for the future brightened?

> *We succeed only as we identify in life, or in war,*
> *or in anything else, a single overriding objective,*
> *and make all considerations bend to that one objective.*
>
> Dwight D. Eisenhower

Barriers to Innovation

Just as there are a variety of ways to enhance and build an innovative organization, there are many ways to turn off innovation. And it is always easier to turn off the innovative process than it is to start it up. Here are 25 barriers to innovation to avoid.

1. Poor planning, direction, and control
2. "Fat" organization with "extra resources"
3. Abundance of personnel
4. Management's lack of commitment to innovation
5. Poor communication
6. Inadequate technology transfer
7. Insufficient technology building
8. Autocratic management
9. Poor working conditions
10. Mismatch of technical skills
11. Unclear work objectives
12. Ineffective performance and development processes for employees
13. Tolerating poor performers and poor performance
14. Working with technologies that are not state-of-the-art

15. Poor reward and recognition programs

16. No dual-ladder system for rewarding the nonmanagement employees

17. Inequities between functions or groups of personnel

18. Inability to interact with customers or to determine their needs

19. Poor communication and coordination between laboratory, manufacturing, and marketing

20. Complex approval systems and excessive red tape

21. Internal politics and gamesmanship

22. Poor leveraging with external sources of technology or information

23. Parochial attitudes and plans

24. Out-of-date management and management training

25. Inadequate or poor facilities and equipment

3M Innovation Wheel

No mathematical formula or scientific process can produce innovation with the algebraic certainty of A:B as C:D. If any rule applies, it is perhaps that interesting and fairly recent theory that order exists in chaos.

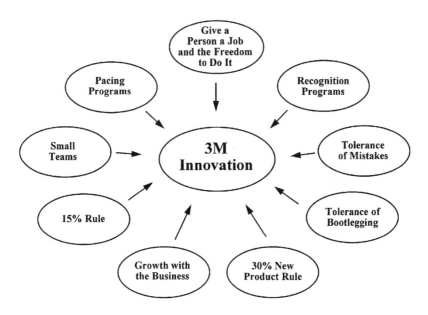

Figure 6. 3M innovation wheel (© 3M)

Every instance of innovation is like a kaleidoscopic image; no two instances are precisely alike. However, we can define some of the contributing factors to innovation. 3M uses this *innovation wheel* to assay its projects and procedures for innovation.

While all these factors *contribute* to innovation, one is preeminent: "Give a person a job and the freedom to do it." Getting out of the way of innovators often is the best thing you can do to and for them. It follows also that you must tolerate their mistakes and going outside of channels. (When he was 3M chairman, Lewis W. Lehr once asked about the amount of *bootlegging* that occurred in a project put together quickly and without formal budgeting. He chuckled when he heard this answer, "There is, sir, such a thing as educating a chairman beyond his need to know." The point of the story is that this practice of grabbing the help you need, even when it's not authorized, is something encouraged from the top.

As shown on the wheel, it is also important to set targets against which to measure progress and results, to focus on those special opportunities that we at 3M call Pacing Programs, and to recognize innovative contributions.

FURTHER READING

M. Barrier. "Innovation As a Way of Life." *Nation's Business* (July 1994): 18–25.

John Seely Brown, "Research that Reinvents the Corporation," *Harvard Business Review* (January–February 1991).

James M. Higgins, *101 Creative Problem Solving Techniques*. New York: The New Management, 1994.

W. G. Howard and B. R. Guile, *Profiting From Innovation* New York: The Free Press, 1992.

T. Kuezmarski, "Inspiring and Implementing the Innovation Mind-Set," *Planning Review* (September/October 1994): 37–38.

D. McKee, "An Organizational Learning Approach to Product Innovation," *Journal of Product Innovation Management*. (New York: Elsevier, September, 1992): 232–245.

Michael Michalko, *Thinkertoys*, Berkeley: Ten Speed Press, 1991.

Willard J. Zangwill, *Lightening Strategies for Innovation*, New York: Lexington Books, 1993.

About the Author

Dr. David P. Sorensen received his B.S. in Chemistry (1952) and Ph.D. in Organic Chemistry (1955) from the University of Utah. After two years with the research laboratories of the M. W. Kellogg Company, Jersey City, New Jersey, he joined 3M's Duplicating Product Division Laboratory in 1957, as a Senior Research Chemist. While in Duplicating Products, he held the positions of Supervisor and Research Specialist. In 1964, he was named Photoeffects Manager in the Imaging Research Laboratory, Central Research Laboratories, and Director of that laboratory in 1967. In August 1971, he became Technical Director, Printing Products Division Laboratory. In January 1981, he was named to the position of Director, Technology Analysis, Corporate Technical Planning and Coordination. In July 1989, he was named Executive Director, Corporate Technical Planning and Coordination. He retired from 3M in 1995. Sorensen is a member of the American Chemical Society, the American Management Association, Phi Kappa Phi, and Phi Beta Kappa.

Dr. David P. Sorensen, 4140 Lakewood Avenue, White Bear Lake, MN 55110